They Came in Chains

The Story of the Slave Ships

GREAT JOURNEYS

They Came in Chains

The Story of the Slave Ships

by Milton Meltzer

BENCHMARK BOOKS

MARSHALL CAVENDISH
NEW YORK

With thanks to Peter P. Hinks, Lecturer, Yale University,
for his careful reading of this manuscript.

Benchmark Books
Marshall Cavendish Corporation
99 White Plains Road
Tarrytown, NY 10591-9001

Cover photograph: *Slaves are ferried from the African coast to the ship that
will carry them across the Atlantic.*

Photo Research by Candlepants Incorporated
Cover Photo: The Granger Collection, New York
The photographs in this book are used by permission and through the courtesy of;
The Granger Collection, New York: 2-3, 14, 23, 27, 28, 32, 42, 44, 46, 52, 54,
55, 58, 59, 66, 67, 70, 72, 76, 77, 78, 79. *Corbis-Bettmann*: 8, 20, 25(left & Right),
29, 34, 36, 47, 57, 62, 71, 84, 85, 88. *The St. Louis Art Museum*: 10.
Archive Photos: 12, 15, 18. *General Research Division, The New York Public Library, Astor,
Lenox and Tilden Foundation*: 16. *Mansell/Time Inc.*: 39. © *Collection of the New York
Historical Society*: 81. *UPI/Corbis Bettmann*: 82, 87.

Library of Congress Cataloging-in-Publication Data
Meltzer, Milton, date.
They came in chains : the story of the slave ships / Milton Meltzer.
p.   cm. — (Great journeys)
Includes bibliographical references and index.
Summary: Describes the history and practice of slavery, particularly the African slave
trade—its origins, growth, and demise from the fifteenth through the nineteenth centuries.
ISBN 0-7614-0967-X (lib. bdg.)
1. Slavery—United States—History—Juvenile literature. 2. Slave trade—United States—
History—Juvenile literature. 3. Slavery—America—History—Juvenile literature. 4. Slave
trade—America—History—Juvenile literature. 5. Slaves—United States—Social condi-
tions—Juvenile literature. 6. Slaves—America—Social conditions—Juvenile literature. [1.
Slavery—History. 2. Slave trade—History.] I. Title. II. Series: Great journeys (Benchmark
Books (Firm))
E446.M48   2000   382'.44—dc21   98-47456   CIP   AC

Printed in the United States

1 3 5 6 4 2

Contents

Also by Milton Meltzer

African-American History: Four Centuries of Black Life
(with Langston Hughes)

Slavery: A World History

Frederick Douglass: In His Own Words

Langston Hughes: A Biography

Carl Sandburg: A Biography

Witches and Witch-Hunts: A History of Persecution

Weapons and Warfare: From the Stone Age to the Space Age

Ten Queens: Portraits of Women of Power

Underground Man

The Black Americans: A History in Their Own Words

Foreword

"The greatest and most fateful migration in history"
—The modern historian Basil Davidson, writing about the slave trade.

MIGRATIONS ARE THE MOVEMENTS OF PEOPLE FROM ONE PLACE TO ANOTHer, with the intent of settling down in a new country or region. In the fifth century A.D., out of the steppes of Asia swept a great mass of people called Huns, who would occupy a large part of central and eastern Europe. A million Irish fled their famine-stricken land in the 1840s to make a new life in North America. Forty years later, at first in a trickle, then in a torrent, four million Jews would turn their backs on poverty and persecution in Eastern Europe to seek refuge in the United States.

But all these people *wished* to change their lives, *wished* to leave home, *wished* to build a new life in what they hoped would be a better place.

"The greatest and most fateful migration in history" was vastly different. It was a *forced* migration. Between the fifteenth and the nineteenth centuries perhaps 20 million African men, women, and children were

An African father is torn away from his wife and child so they can be sold separately.

captured, bought, or kidnapped by European and American slave traders and sold to labor on the plantations and in the mines of the Americas.

All of us, in some way, are connected to that shameful history. For it is quite likely that just about every one of us is descended from slaves. No matter what our color or where in the world we came from, we have ancestors who at one time or another were slaves. Many were slaves at one time and masters at another.

How slavery arose, what its consequences were—in Africa, in Europe, and in America—will be told here. Not in great detail, for that would take many volumes, but in its broad aspects.

I have often relied on original sources, on diaries, memoirs, letters, documents, and eyewitness accounts, using wherever possible the words of the people who lived this history. I have taken the liberty of shortening some long passages and have modernized spelling and punctuation for easier reading. The language itself, however, appears in these pages unchanged.

A note: The sea-lane across the Atlantic followed by the slave ships from the coast of Africa to the ports of the Americas was known as the Middle Passage. It was called this because it was the central stretch of the triangle of trade. The legs of the triangle were the voyages from Europe to Africa, from Africa to the Western Hemisphere, and back to Europe.

A stone carving depicts an African captive from Ethiopia destined for slavery in Egypt. The Egyptians enslaved prisoners of war long before the West African slave trade began.

One

An Ancient Practice

In 1442—FIFTY YEARS BEFORE COLUMBUS LANDED IN AMERICA—A LITTLE Portuguese ship captured twelve blacks in a raid on the Atlantic coast of Africa. The prisoners were carried back to Lisbon to become the slaves of Prince Henry the Navigator.

The European slave trade had begun.

Those victims were black. They were neither the first nor the last. Nor were they the only people of color to be enslaved. People had been enslaved before this, and slavery would continue for many generations to come, even to the present day.

What does it mean to be enslaved? When a human being is owned by another and is made to do compulsory, unpaid labor, that person is a slave. The owner might be an ordinary person or a king, a queen, a noble, a tribe, a government, the clergy, or a business. Like a horse, the slave can be bought, sold, hired out, exchanged, given as a gift, or even inherited.

11

Prince Henry of Portugal (1394–1460). Called the Navigator, he founded a school of navigation and sent his ships down the coast of West Africa in search of profit. His sailors brought back the first African slaves from that region.

The slave has no rights at all. The law considers the slave to be property, with which the owner can do anything he likes. To work as long and as hard as the owner desires, at any kind of task, and for nothing more than the food needed to keep the slave alive. For in the master's eyes, the slave is nothing more than a thing.

Slavery started a long time ago, in the early history of humankind. It was not the invention of any one mind. (Few things are.) It probably grew up in many places in response to certain conditions. Most often it seems to have been the cause or the result of warfare. One group or tribe raided another, captured the people, and spared the prisoners' lives so that they could be made to work or replace members of the family lost in battle. When farmers or shepherds could produce more food than they needed, why not use the extra amount to feed the people they had captured? Better than to kill them, for the victors could make the losers do their work at little cost to themselves. So, slavery became a tool of production.

The evidence unearthed by archaeologists digging into the soil of ancient buried cities shows that slavery was practiced ten thousand years ago—among the people of ancient Babylon and Assyria, Egypt, Palestine, China, Greece, Rome, and in Africa too.

The people of Africa had kept slaves themselves long before the Europeans reached their shores. At the time the foreign slave trade began, Africa had a population of about 100 million. This huge continent, over three times as big as the United States, ranked next to Asia in size. The people were as diverse as the contours of the land. Hundreds of languages, belonging to a few great language families, were spoken. The sheer vastness of Africa makes it impossible to generalize easily about it.

Most Africans lived in small communities. Farming and herding made most people self-sufficient. Yet they also had a wide range of handicraft industries and highly developed art forms. There were cities of considerable size, markets for the exchange of goods, a recognized means of exchange through cowrie shells, and a system of taxation.

All these peoples in Africa belonged to many smaller groups, welded together by a long process of conquest into kingdoms ruled by royal families. Then came the common people, and below them, the slaves. The Africans had military organizations, capitals, and courts, and as in most societies, wars of conquest were common.

Like other people throughout the world, the Africans had practiced slavery since prehistoric times. They took prisoners of war and forced them into slavery. They bought slaves from one another. In certain regions of the Congo, for instance, there were large numbers of villagers enslaved to members of the aristocracy. In some places it was the custom to sell people condemned as thieves or murderers. The punishment for adultery, too, was slavery.

The ravages of war and the protracted famine caused by drought or locust plagues could drive a person in desperation to sell another. An observer, Filippo Pigafetta, describes such a crisis in 1591:

The populations, which were reduced to wandering in these regions, starved to death. . . . A small quantity of food came to cost as much as one slave. Driven by necessity, father sold son, brother sold brother, so desperately did each try to procure food for himself, by no matter what villainy. . . . The sellers said that they were slaves, and those who were sold as such confirmed it, in order to be delivered from the torment of hunger.

An African artist made this bronze head of a king from the court of Benin.

Arabs, long before 300 B.C., had organized a flourishing slave trade along the east coast of Africa.

The trade routes that crisscrossed Africa supplied local markets with slaves as well as ivory, copper, silks, and metalware. The trade was fed in part by the wars African kingdoms waged among themselves. However, such wars, usually local and small, produced few captives.

In Dahomey (now Benin) more upper-class people—nobles, priests, and soothsayers—were enslaved than commoners. This happened sometimes when the accession of a new king was disputed by a brother. In the struggle for power the loser, along with his family and supporters, was enslaved. Sometimes stronger states would force weaker ones to supply a certain number of slaves to them every year. In some areas people lived in terror of becoming the victims of raids and kidnappings.

The slaves of an African ruler bow down before him on a ceremonial occasion.

There were still other ways in which enslavement came about. People, usually children, were given as security to guarantee a loan or sold as compensation to cancel a debt. As in other times and places, slavery was deeply rooted in African society. It was a motive for war, a commodity for long-range trading, an instrument of law and justice, and a badge of prestige.

Yet generally, as long as greed was not a driving force, slavery in Africa did not lead to violence or the abuse of power. Old slaves long associated with the master's family were treated with respect and sometimes became confidants or representatives of the chief. For recently acquired slaves, this was not so. The slave was always a piece of property passed on by inheritance, and the master could dispose of him as he chose. Yet the owner was likely to treat him properly for fear of public disapproval.

Slaves were used for agricultural labor, on construction projects, and for household drudgery. In the Congo they were the bulk of the male working class, for a freeman would not work on the land or as a paid servant. In some of the larger kingdoms, slave workers were driven inhumanely, much as Africans would later be driven on the plantations and in the mines of the Western Hemisphere.

In the Songhay Kingdom of the fifteenth century, according to Basil Davidson, "'slaves' tended to form occupational castes: They became blacksmiths, boat-builders, stablemen, makers of songs, bodyguards of their sovereign lord." They were the majority of the population, and their social condition was really little different from that of free peasants or artisans.

The scholar R. S. Rattray, who studied the Ashanti, a forest people, found that among them a slave could marry, own property, and even become his master's heir. In many cases a slave became an adopted member of the family. And in time, such descendants so merged and intermarried with the owner's kinfolk that only a few would know their

Slaves carry a high-ranking person in the kingdom of the Congo.

origin. African society was fluid enough for a captive to move up the ladder from slave to freeman and even to chief. The slave was not a person permanently imprisoned in servitude, with little or no hope of liberation.

Nevertheless, the fact that African slavery was different in its origins and in its effects should not blind us to the truth: it was still the exploitation and subjugation of human beings. Not all slaves accepted their condition. They sometimes resisted, as slaves have everywhere from the evidence of the earliest historical records. Slaves tried to escape tyranny by fleeing and founding separate hamlets at a distance, in dense forests, mountains, or swamps. Or they might place themselves under the protection of another authority who had promised to set them free. And in extreme cases, slaves rose up in bloody rebellions.

limited demand for slaves, nor did other European countries ask for them. The profit on other goods was more appealing, perhaps amounting to more than ten times the capital invested in a voyage.

So small was the European need for slaves that in 1623 an English ship captain refused slaves offered him on the coast. When an African showed him "certain young black women which he told me were slaves," he replied, "We were a people who did not deal in such commodities, neither do we buy or sell one another." The French in 1571 specifically condemned trade in slaves, with the royal declaration that "France, mother of liberty, permits no slaves."

Had nothing else happened, the small slave trade might have dwindled away. But the course of history was radically changed when the Western Hemisphere was colonized by the European powers. From its onset until late in the nineteenth century—a period of nearly four hundred years—millions of African captives were forcibly transported from their homeland across the Atlantic.

The first voyage of Christopher Columbus to America in 1492 had tremendous, far-reaching effects on the Atlantic slave trade. As he claimed possession of the lands he mistakenly thought were part of Asia, he was greeted by the native people he called Indians. He wrote to his sponsors, the king and queen of Spain, that the Indians "would make fine servants. . . . Should your Majesties command it, all the inhabitants could be taken away to Castile, or made slaves on the island."

Columbus saw the people of the Americas as inferior beings, ripe for enslavement. And their lands? Prizes to be seized and exploited. The European invaders who followed him quickly began to reap wealth from the rich natural resources of the thinly populated Caribbean islands and the Central and South American mainland.

Every export crop—sugar, rice, coffee, tobacco, cotton—on the plantations of the New World required large-scale production. And plenty of cheap labor in order to be profitable. The Indians were forced into slave

Christopher Columbus, landing on the island of Hispaniola in 1492, notes that the native people "are fit to be ordered about and made to work." He captured Indians and sent hundreds to Spain to be sold in Seville's slave market.

labor in the mines and on the plantations of the European colonizers. The conditions were intolerable, and many fled or revolted. Death became wholesale. The Indians died quickly of the harsh labor, brutal treatment, and the white man's diseases, against which they had no immunity.

When the whites ran short of Indian labor they turned to Africa. They knew that slaves could be bought on its western coast. Charles V, king of Spain, agreed that black slaves would be useful and granted an *asiento*, a license to import slaves from Africa to the New World. By 1540, ten thousand slaves a year were being carried in chains across the Atlantic to the West Indies, while others were taken to South America and Mexico.

Soon English sea captains broke into the Spanish and Portuguese monopoly. In 1562 John Hawkins—called "admiral" by some, "pirate" by others—led three ships to the coast of Guinea. On that first voyage he took a shortcut by robbing a Portuguese slave ship of its human cargo. Two years later he got financing from his queen, Elizabeth I. Gratified by the profits his slaving brought her, she rewarded him with a knighthood. In 1567, on a third voyage, he obtained 470 slaves as booty. In exchange, he had loaned his crewmen as mercenaries to two African kings battling rival kingdoms.

Hawkins's young cousin, Francis Drake, joined him in slaving voyages and later made himself independently wealthy through slaving and piracy. He too was knighted by Elizabeth.

As the Portuguese monopoly on the slave trade was broken, other nations entered the market. The Dutch pushed the Portuguese off the African coast in 1642, and by the 1700s the English and French, despite their earlier objections, had surpassed the Dutch to become the two leading competitors in the trafficking of slaves. In the late 1700s, Europeans were operating forty slave stations on the coast. In the end the British outstripped all their rivals to take more than half the total trade.

The entire shore along the Gulf of Guinea was often called the Slave

Sir John Hawkins, one of England's early slave ship captains, named his *flagship the* Jesus of Lubeck.

On one of his slaving voyages, Sir Francis Drake commanded a ship called the Grace of God.

Coast. The coastline along what is now Ghana was also known as the Gold Coast, due to its inland deposits of gold. It was this precious metal, along with the lure of human cargo, that drew the European colonists.

The African merchants adapted themselves to the new demand for slaves. They were eager to have Europe's manufactured goods. Each European nation supplied its coastal stations with its own goods. These included such valued items as guns and gunpowder, glass beads, alcohol, cutlasses, machetes, iron bars, gold-braided cocked hats, copper kettles and basins, cottons, taffeta, silk, and looking glasses. The trade on the African side was run by kings and nobles and wealthy merchants. When the inland people were at war with those nearer the sea, the traders could provide great numbers of slaves of all ages. In 1681 an English slaver boasted he got three hundred slaves "almost for nothing" because one nation had just beaten another and had taken a large number of prisoners. At other times slaves might be scarce because there were too many ships on the coast or because the Africans were at peace.

But as demand for slaves increased, the hunger for slave profits led to a great rise in warfare. Each tribe's wealth was fattened by the number of captives it took. The great majority of slaves came from West Africa, along the three thousand miles of coast from Senegal in the north to Angola in the south. Some, but not many, came from East Africa. A large share of captives belonged to the peoples living in what are now Benin, Ghana, and Nigeria. Few slaves came from the coastal peoples. Protecting their own, they bought or captured people inland, and in turn these Africans supplied themselves with people still farther east.

Africans sold slaves for guns, which were used to take still more slaves. As the slave trade flourished, chiefs and kings extended the list of crimes that called for enslavement. Almost any offense might serve when profit was the motive.

One English trader, James Perry of Liverpool, testified in 1789 that 14,000 slaves were exported every year from the Niger River delta. In

The Arabs bought up slaves by the thousands at this slave market in Zanzibar, an island off Africa's eastern coast.

just one trading station on the Guinea coast, as many as forty to fifty European ships loaded slaves each year. A great many victims of this trade were children.

Slaves from the interior were brought to the coast in coffles. Men, women, and children might be marched hundreds of miles to the sea, facing great hazards along the way—lions, crocodiles, raiders, epidemics.

What was it like to be stripped of your freedom and marched in chains to some unknown destination? Mungo Park, a young Scottish surgeon, told of traveling in 1797 with a coffle of seventy-three slaves for a distance of five hundred miles. It took two months for them to reach the

Coffles of slaves—men, women, and children—are marched from Africa's interior to be sold on the coast.

mouth of the Gambia River. Many of the slaves kept asking him if his countrymen were cannibals:

A deeply rooted idea that the whites purchase Negroes for the purpose of devouring them, or of selling them to others, that they may be devoured hereafter, naturally makes the slaves contemplate a journey toward the coast with great terror, insomuch that the Slavers are forced to keep them constantly in irons, and watch them very closely to prevent their escape. They are commonly secured by putting the right leg of one and the left of another into the same pair of fetters. By supporting the fetters with a string, they can walk, though very slowly. Every four slaves are likewise fastened together by the necks with a strong rope or twisted thongs; and in the night an additional pair of fetters is put on their hands, and sometimes a light chain passed around their necks.

Such of them as evince marks of discontent, are secured in a different manner. A thick billet of wood is cut about three feet long, and a smooth notch being made upon one side of it, the

Shackles and fetters used to confine captives aboard ship.

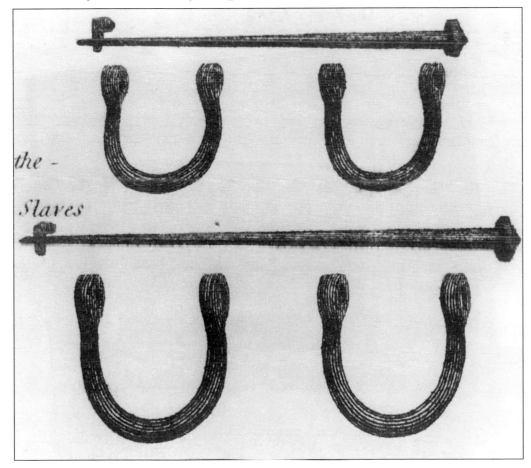

ankle of the slave is bolted to the smooth part by means of a strong iron staple, one prong of which passes on each side of the ankle.

As those caravans of shackled men, women, and children were marched down to the roads, river mouths, and harbors along that immense coast, they left behind them evidence of their ghastly journey, as described by a British naval officer, Captain Joseph Denham. He had served on the west coast station and had ridden along the trail slave caravans took. This is what he told a Parliamentary committee:

The ground around the well at Meshroo [in Fezzan] is strewed with human skeletons of the slaves who have arrived exhausted with thirst and fatigue. Round the spot are lying more than one hundred skeletons, some of them with skin still remaining attached to the bones. We bivouacked in the midst of these remains of the victims of avarice after a long day's journey of twenty-six miles in which one of our party had counted 109 of the skeletons. . . .

While I was dozing on my horse about noon near the wells of Omah, overcome by the heat of the sun, I was suddenly awoke by crashing under my feet which startled me excessively; I found that my steed had without alarm stepped upon the perfect skeletons of two human beings, cracking their brittle bones, and by one trip of his foot separating a skull from the trunk, which rolled on like a ball before him.

Those slaves who survived that ordeal and arrived on the coast were traded to the Europeans. But before the Europeans could bargain for slaves they had to buy the king's own stock of slaves at a set price, usually higher than the regular price. Then they could begin bargaining with

How Did Slave Traders Justify Their Actions?

Shortly after the Portuguese began the European slave trade by raiding for blacks on the African coast, Prince Henry asked the Pope to approve more raids. The Pope's reply granted "to all of those who shall be engaged in the said war, complete forgiveness of all their sins." In 1455 a papal bull, or declaration, authorized Portugal to reduce to servitude all non-Christian peoples.

The Church did its best to keep Christians from becoming the slaves of infidels (non-Christians). But this ban did not extend to unbelievers. They were thought not to deserve freedom. If infidels were enslaved by Christians, new souls would be procured for the Church to convert. So slavery was seen as a weapon to extend Christianity, and as a deserved punishment for pagans and heretics.

In the New World colonies established by Spain and Portugal the clergy themselves owned thousands of slaves. That, to many minds, made the African slave trade legitimate.

In a way, this was like the rationale some Africans gave themselves when they chose not to enslave people of their own community, but only those so-called "strangers," or "outsiders." But merchants—European or African—who handled thousands of slaves, could not have cared less about the religion or origin of their commodities.

A slave pen, called a barracoon, on the Solyma River in Sierra Leone.

his subjects of lower rank. In addition, the king levied the value of twenty slaves on each ship as a port duty.

Price was influenced by the quality of the human merchandise. Willem Bosman, a Dutch trader, told in a letter of 1700 how costs were determined at Fida, on the Dahomey coast:

When these slaves come to Fida, they are put in prison all together, and when we treat concerning buying them, they are all brought together in a large plain; where, by our surgeons, whose province it is, they are thoroughly examined, even to the smallest member, and that naked too both men and women, without the least distinction or modesty. Those which are approved as good are set on one side; and the lame or faulty are set by as invalids, which are here called Mackrons. These are such as are above five-and-thirty years old, or are maimed in the arms, legs, hand or feet, have lost a tooth, are grey-haired, or have films over their eyes; as well as all those which are affected with diseases.

The invalids and the maimed being thrown out . . . the remainder are numbered, and it is entered who delivered them. In the meanwhile a burning iron, with the arms or name of the companies, lies in the fire; with which ours are marked on the breast. . . .

The price for the women was usually 20 to 25 percent less than for the men. They were branded on the buttock, not the breast. After the branding, a smell of burned flesh hung in the air.

An English slaver of the same period, Captain Thomas Phillips, said his surgeons had to be wary of being cheated or fooled by tricks used to conceal defects in the merchandise.

Then the cappasheirs [African traders] each brought out his slaves according to his degree and quality, the greatest first, etc., and our surgeons examined them well in all kinds to see that they were sound in wind and limb, making them jump, stretch out their arms swiftly, looking in their mouths to judge of their age; for the cappasheirs are so cunning that they shave them all close before we see them, so that let them be ever so old we can see no grey hairs on their heads or beards; and then having liquor'd them well and sleeked with palm oil, 'tis no easy matter to know an old one from a middle-aged one, but by the teeth's decay. But [o]ur greatest care of all is to buy none that are pox'd, lest they should infect the rest aboard.

The price of slaves depended on the age and condition of the slave, as we have seen. But also on the period of slaving and the location of the trading post. At times a slaver had to call at several ports before gathering enough slaves to make up the desired cargo.

On the day set for sailing to the New World, the slaves were given a full meal, the signal of their last hours in their homeland. Then, chained in pairs at the ankles, they were moved onto the slave ships. As they came aboard, they were stripped naked (for cleanliness, the captains said) and the men and women put into separate compartments.

It was time to sail. . . .

Slaves brought to the coast by African traders are examined for their physical condition before purchase.

A slave dealer auctions off Africans to prospective buyers, who will then ship them to the Americas.

Three

An African Boy
Kidnapped

WHAT DID AFRICANS THINK AND FEEL WHEN THEY WERE FORCED ON board a slave ship? Personal accounts are rare. Perhaps the best of the memoirs left to us was written by Olaudah Equiano (also known as Gustavus Vassa). He was born in what is now Nigeria in 1745. At the age of eleven he was kidnapped and sold into slavery. Later he was sold again—and again—to a Virginia planter, then to a British naval officer, and finally to a Philadelphia merchant who gave him the chance to buy his freedom in 1777. He made his living as a sailor and became active in the antislavery movement in England. In 1789 he published his autobiography. It contained these passages describing his voyage as a young slave on the Middle Passage to America:

The first object which saluted my eyes when I arrived on the coast was the sea, and a slave ship, which was then riding at anchor, and waiting for its cargo. These filled me with astonishment, which was soon connected with terror, when I was carried on board. I was immediately handled, and tossed up, to see if I were sound, by some of the crew; and I was now persuaded that I had gotten into a world of bad spirits, and that they were going to kill me. Their complexions too, differing so much from ours, their long hair, and the language they spoke (which was very different from any I had ever heard), united to confirm me in this belief.

Indeed, such were the horrors of my views and fears at the moment, that, if ten thousand worlds had been my own, I would have freely parted with them all to have exchanged my condition with that of the meanest slave in my own country. When I looked around the ship too and saw a large furnace or copper boiling, and a multitude of black people of every description chained together, every one of their countenances expressing dejection and sorrow, I no longer doubted of my fate; and, quite overpowered with horror and anguish, I fell motionless on the deck and fainted . . . .

When I recovered a little, I found some black people about me who, I believed, were some of those who had brought me on board, and had been receiving their pay; they talked to me in order to cheer me, but all in vain. I asked them if I were not to be eaten by those white men with horrible looks, red faces and loose hair. They told me I was not; and one of the crew brought me a small portion of spiritous liquor in a wine glass; but being afraid of him, I would not take it out of his hand. One of the blacks therefore took it from him and gave it to me, and I took a little down my palate, which, instead of reviving me, as they thought it would, threw me into the greatest consternation at the strange feeling it produced, having never tasted any such liquor before.

Soon after this, the blacks who brought me on board went off, and left me abandoned to despair. I now saw myself deprived of all chance of returning to my native country, or even the least

Fettered blacks on the west coast of Africa are taken aboard ship for the Middle Passage across the Atlantic to the slave markets of the Americas.

glimpse of hope of gaining the shore, which I now considered as friendly; and I even wished for my former slavery in preference to my present situation, which was filled with horrors of every kind, still heightened by my ignorance of what I was to undergo.

I was not long suffered to indulge my grief; I was soon put down under the decks, and there I received such a salutation in my nostrils as I had never experienced in my life: so that with the loathsomeness of the stench and crying together, I became so sick and low that I was not able to eat, nor had I the least desire to taste anything.

I now wished for the last friend, death, to relieve me; but

The crew of a slave ship stows the human "merchandise" below deck at sunset. Note the club, knife, and whip, always present to quell rebellion.

soon, to my grief, two of the white men offered me eatables; and, on my refusing to eat, one of them held me fast by the hands, and laid me across, I think, the windlass, and tied my feet, while the other flogged me severely.

I had never experienced anything of this kind before; and although, not being used to the water, I naturally feared that element the first time I saw it, yet nevertheless, could I have got over the nettings, I would have jumped over the side, but I could not; and, besides, the crew used to watch us very closely who were not chained down to the decks, lest we should leap into the water; and I have seen some of these poor African prisoners most severely cut for attempting to do so, and hourly whipped for not eating. This indeed was often the case with myself.

In a little time after, amongst the poor chained men, I found some of my own nation, which in a small degree gave ease to my mind. I inquired of these what was to be done with us. They gave me to understand we were to be carried to these white people's country to work for them. I then was a little revived, and thought, if it were no worse than working, my situation was not so desperate. . . .

Almost everything that happened made the boy more fearful. He showed again and again how cruel the whites could be:

But still I feared I should be put to death, the white people looked and acted, as I thought, in so savage a manner; for I had never seen among any people such instances of brutal cruelty; and this not only shown towards us blacks, but also to some of the whites.

One white man in particular I saw, when we were permitted to be on deck, flogged so unmercifully with a large rope near the foremast, that he died in consequence of it; and they tossed him over the side as they would have done a brute. This made me fear these people the more; and I expected nothing less than to be treated in the same manner. . . .

One day they had taken a number of fishes; and when they had killed and satisfied themselves with as many as they thought fit, to our astonishment who were on the deck, rather than give any of them to us to eat, as we expected, they tossed the remaining fish into the sea again, although we begged and prayed for some as well

as we could, but in vain. Some of my countrymen, being pressed by hunger, took an opportunity, when they thought no one saw them, of trying to get a little privately; but they were discovered, and the attempt procured them some very severe floggings.

When the ship had taken in all its cargo, the slaves were stowed below deck, so that they could not see how the ship was managed. Equiano tells of the conditions in the hold:

The stench of the hold while we were on the coast was so intolerably loathsome that it was dangerous to remain there for any time, and some of us had been permitted to stay on the deck for the fresh air; but now that the whole ship's cargo was confined together, it became absolutely pestilential.

The closeness of the place, and the heat of the climate, added to the number in the ship, which was so crowded that each had scarcely room to turn himself, almost suffocated us. This produced copious perspirations, so that the air soon became unfit for respiration, from a variety of loathsome smells, and brought on a sickness among the slaves, of which many died, thus falling victims to the improvident avarice, as I may call it, of their purchasers.

This wretched situation was again aggravated by the galling of the chains, now become insupportable; and the filth of the neces-

---

In 1860 the slave ship Wildfire *was captured by an American naval vessel off the coast of Cuba and brought to Key West, Florida. The ship was in violation of American laws against the slave trade. It was carrying 510 Africans purchased on the Congo River. Fifty of the slaves were adult males; about four hundred were boys between the ages of ten and sixteen. Below deck were about sixty women and young girls. More than ninety other Africans had died during the voyage. An American officer daguerreotyped (produced a photograph on a silver plate) the captives crowded on the deck. This engraving was made from that daguerreotype.*

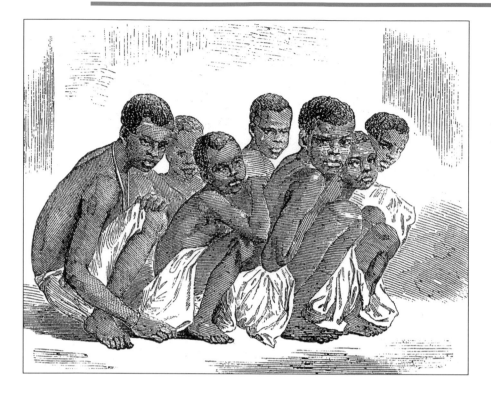

A detail from a drawing shows how slaves were crowded together below deck. In such conditions the spread of deadly dysentery was almost inevitable.

sary tubs, into which the children often fell, and were almost suffocated. The shrieks of the women, and the groans of the dying, rendered the whole a scene of horror almost inconceivable.

Happily perhaps for myself I was soon reduced so low here that it was thought necessary to keep me almost always on deck; and from my extreme youth I was not put in fetters. In this situation I expected every hour to share the fate of my companions, some of whom were almost daily brought upon deck at the point of death, which I began to hope would soon put an end to my miseries. Often did I think many of the inhabitants of the deep much more happy than myself, I envied them the freedom they enjoyed, and as often wished I could change my condition for theirs. . . .

So desperate and hopeless did the Africans become that some chose the only way out:

One day, when we had a smooth sea and moderate wind, two of my wearied countrymen who were chained together (I was near them at the time), preferring death to such a life of misery, somehow made through the nettings and jumped into the sea; immediately another quite dejected fellow, who on account of his illness was suffered to be out of irons, also followed their example; and I believe many more would very soon have done the same if they had not been prevented by the ship's crew who were instantly alarmed.

Those of us that were the most active were in the moment put down under the deck, and there was such a noise and confusion amongst the people of the ship as I never heard before, to stop her, and get the boat out to go after the slaves. However two of the wretches were drowned, but they got the other, and afterwards flogged him unmercifully for thus attempting to prefer death to slavery.

Would the vast ocean never come to a shore? Then one day they came in sight of the West Indies island of Barbados:

The whites on board gave a great shout, and made many signs of joy to us. We did not know what to think of this; but as the vessel drew nearer we plainly saw the harbour, and other ships of different kinds and sizes; and we soon anchored amongst them off Bridge-Town.

Many merchants and planters now came on board, though it was in the evening. They put us in separate parcels, and examined us attentively. They also made us jump, and pointed to the land, signifying we were to go there. We thought by this we should be eaten by these ugly men, as they appeared to us; and, when soon after we were all put down under the deck again, there was much dread and trembling.

*By 1842 almost all the maritime powers had declared the Atlantic slave trade illegal.
But the law was ignored for many years. When the British Royal Navy patrolling the
seas in 1846 captured a Spanish slave ship and freed the Africans, an officer painted
this watercolor of the slave quarters.*

Four

Hell on a Slave Ship

WHO WERE THE PEOPLE WHO BROUGHT THE SLAVES FROM AFRICA TO the New World?

A very mixed lot: cutthroats and Christians, speculators and adventurers, gentlemen and pirates, seamen and surgeons. The slave trade was not considered an evil occupation. A man who trafficked in slaves was not shut out of office or honors. Engaged in the British trade were dukes, earls, lords, countesses, kings. Many slaves bought on the African coast were branded with the initials "DY"—for the Duke of York. Mayors of Liverpool were involved in the trade, and slave traders sat in both houses of Parliament.

Or take Henry Laurens of Charleston, South Carolina, who got rich off the slave trade. He was elected president of the Continental Congress during the American Revolution. Later he gave up the slaving business but lamented losing so easy a way of becoming even richer.

An American slave trader in 1830 orders the captive Africans to board his ship for transport to the United States.

There are many examples of people who do good deeds with one hand, and evil deeds with the other. Just as people can create beautiful art and yet do ugly things in their personal life. History has often revealed how contradictory the human character can be. The Englishman Foster Cunliffe, for example, was a pioneer in the slave trade. (It is doubtful, though, that Cunliffe ever crossed the Atlantic in one of his own slave ships.) Yet he is described on his churchyard monument as "a Christian devout and exemplary, friend to mercy, patron to distress, an enemy only to vice and sloth, he lived esteemed by all who knew him, and died lamented by the wise and good."

Men who had taken part in the slave trade sometimes turned against it and provided powerful evidence for the antislavery campaign. One of these was Reverend John Newton. As a young man he had captained a slave ship sailing to the coast of Sierra Leone. Pious always, even though a buyer and seller of human beings, he used to order prayers twice a day on his slave ship, saying that he never knew "sweeter or more frequent hours of divine communion."

While waiting for a coffle of slaves to be delivered to him on the coast, Newton used the time to write the hymn "How Sweet the Name of Jesus Sounds." Later, he left the trade to become an evangelical minister in London. It was then that he wrote the popular hymn "Amazing Grace."

The bishop of London himself once owned 655 slaves and would not free them until the government compensated him for them in 1833. The church supported the slave trade as a means of converting heathens. It looked upon nonwhites as savages in need of the civilizing influence of religion.

Slavery was a fact of life for centuries. People tended to accept what they saw all around them. For a long time even the Quakers—British and American—found it hard to extend their nonconformity to so profitable an enterprise as slave dealing. But by the 1600s Quakers began to question the morality of slavery, and gradually they became active in the abolition movement.

Elizabeth I, Charles II, James II—all were British monarchs who invested in the trade. So, the pillars of the slave trade were also pillars of society, who conducted their trade in human beings with the blessings of the church, the government, the monarchy, and the public.

To take part in the buying of Africans for export required capital, ships, crews, and goods for trading. The first step of the slave trade companies was to find a captain with some experience and the skill to deal in slaves with the chiefs and merchants on the African coast. Officers were hired, along with surgeons, carpenters, sailmakers, and coopers. Some of the seamen were novices—young runaways from home or from apprenticeships, or men just out of prison. Some seamen were kidnapped by "crimping": that is, a ship's captain plotted with an innkeeper, who plied

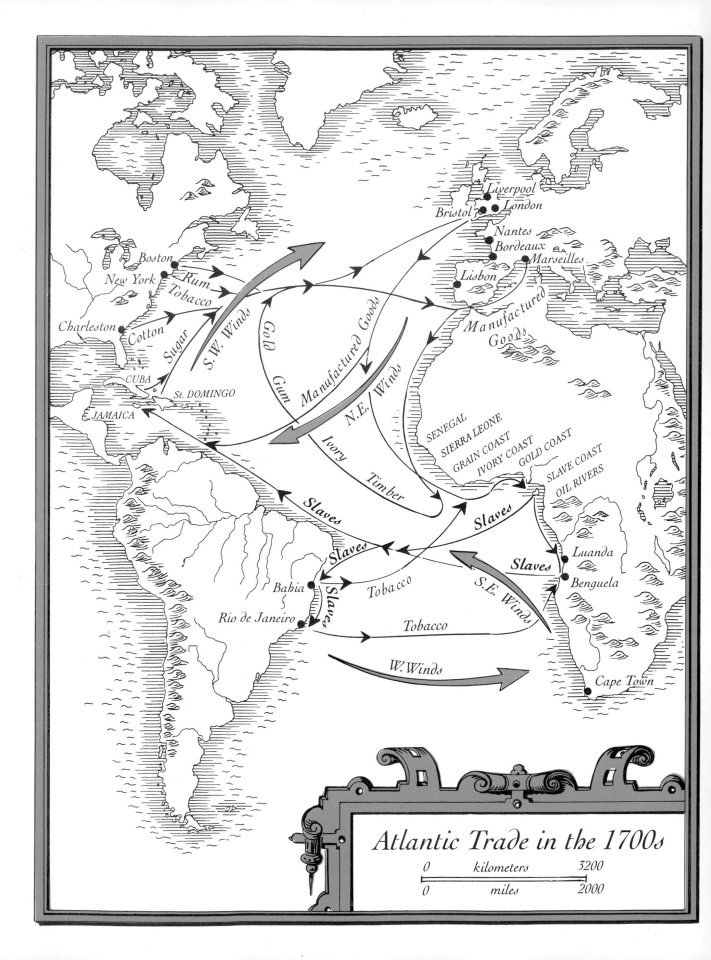

Liverpool
London
Bristol
Nantes
Bordeaux
Marseilles
Lisbon

Manufactured Goods

Boston
New York
Rum
Tobacco
Charleston
Cotton
Sugar
CUBA
St. DOMINGO
JAMAICA

S.W. Winds
Gold
Gum
Manufactured Goods
N.E. Winds
Ivory
Timber

SENEGAL
SIERRA LEONE
GRAIN COAST
IVORY COAST
GOLD COAST
SLAVE COAST
OIL RIVERS

Luanda
Benguela

Slaves
Slaves
Slaves
Slaves
Slaves

Bahia
Rio de Janeiro
Tobacco
Tobacco

S.E. Winds
W. Winds

Cape Town

Atlantic Trade in the 1700s

| 0 | kilometers | 3200 |
| 0 | miles | 2000 |

the penniless young man with liquor at his inn. When dead drunk, he was carried off and tossed on board a slave ship.

As Equiano observed, the seamen were often treated harshly, given poor food, and worked nearly to death. John Newton said, "There is no trade in which seamen are treated with so little humanity." Officers abused sailors as badly as they did the slaves or even worse. For such a trivial offense as breaking his captain's glass, the cabin boy James Morley was suspended by a rope around his hands, flogged and left hanging there for a long time. Captain Colley of Liverpool once flew into a rage, grabbed an iron spike, and beat to death the ship's cook, a seaman, the carpenter, and his mate.

Sailors said their lot was to sleep on deck and die on deck, from hunger, from exhaustion, and from constant beatings. Beyond such suffering, they were required to treat the slaves so viciously that John Newton said it was no wonder that "it gradually brings numbness upon the heart and renders those who are engaged in it too indifferent to the sufferings of their fellow creatures."

What were the physical conditions aboard those ships carrying their human cargoes? The ships were small and undermanned, with crews of rarely more than eighteen men. Living quarters were uniformly slovenly and foul. The height of slave ship decks averaged between four and five feet. Sometimes the ship owners added to the slave holds by building half-decks along the sides of the ship. There the slaves were packed in two rows, one above the other. Only ten to thirteen inches of surface room was allotted each slave. Packed like spoons and unable to stand, they suffered cruelly on the voyages to America. There is a record of one slaver of the 1840s, a tiny vessel of eighteen tons, whose crew consisted of only six Portuguese. It was built with a space of eighteen inches between decks, and was meant to carry two hundred fifty African children, about seven years of age.

Early each morning at sea the slaves were brought up on deck. Their

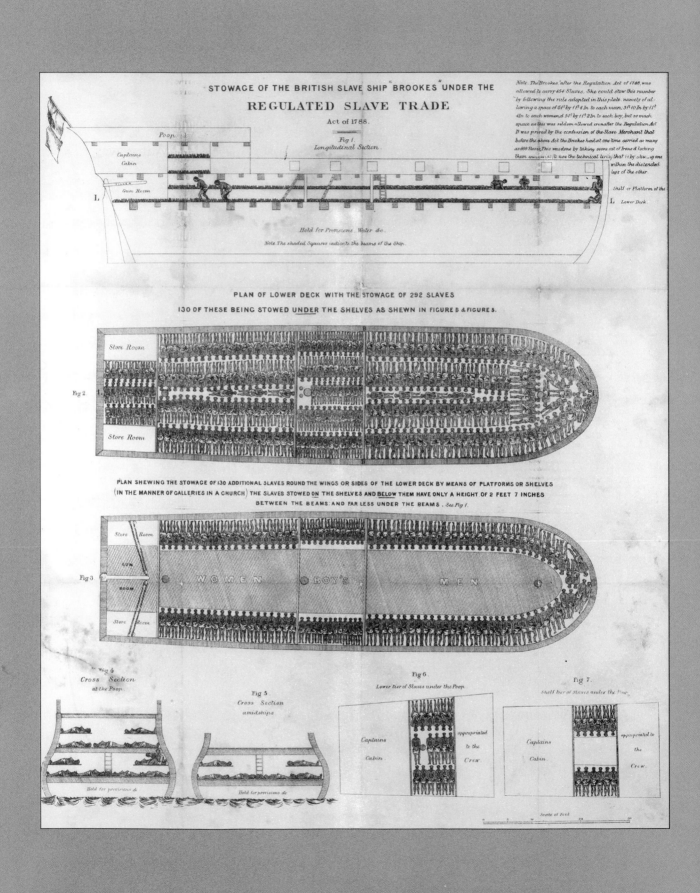

STOWAGE OF THE BRITISH SLAVE SHIP "BROOKES" UNDER THE

REGULATED SLAVE TRADE

Act of 1788.

Fig 1.
Longitudinal Section.

Poop

Captains Cabin

Gun Room

Hold for Provisions, Water &c.

Note. The shaded Squares indicate the beams of the Ship.

Shelf or Platform of the Lower Deck.

PLAN OF LOWER DECK WITH THE STOWAGE OF 292 SLAVES

130 OF THESE BEING STOWED UNDER THE SHELVES AS SHEWN IN FIGURE 6 & FIGURE 5.

Fig 2

Store Room

Store Room

PLAN SHEWING THE STOWAGE OF 130 ADDITIONAL SLAVES ROUND THE WINGS OR SIDES OF THE LOWER DECK BY MEANS OF PLATFORMS OR SHELVES
(IN THE MANNER OF GALLERIES IN A CHURCH) THE SLAVES STOWED ON THE SHELVES AND BELOW THEM HAVE ONLY A HEIGHT OF 2 FEET 7 INCHES
BETWEEN THE BEAMS: AND FAR LESS UNDER THE BEAMS . See Fig 1.

Fig 3

Store Room

GUN ROOM

Store Room

WOMEN   BOY'S   M E N

Fig 4
Cross Section
at the Poop

Fig 5.
Cross Section
amidships

Fig 6.
Lower tier of Slaves under the Poop

Fig 7.
Shelf tier of Slaves under the Poop

Hold for provisions &c

Hold for provisions &c

Captains Cabin   appropriated to the Crew.

Captains Cabin   appropriated to the Crew.

Scale of Feet

irons were examined and a long chain locked to a ring fixed on the deck was run through the rings of the shackles of the men and locked to another ringbolt fixed to the deck. By this method dozens of slaves could be fastened to the chains, preventing any attempt at rebellion. Water was ladled out so the slaves could wash, and the ship's surgeon then looked the men over for sores or sickness.

Food came twice a day, breakfast at ten and another meal at four. It was usually rice, farina, yams, beans, and perhaps bran. Beans boiled into a pulp might be the evening meal. Most slaves loathed this dish and would toss it overboard if not watched. Say grace before meals, the captain insisted, and be sure to give thanks afterward.

If the weather was good, the slaves were forced to sing and dance on deck, making music of their own on a drum or the bottom of a tub. The aim was to exercise them and perhaps lighten their anguish, but the songs they sang were often expressions of grief over loss of their homeland. If slaves refused to exercise, they were whipped to make them jump about. Slaves who were not trusted out of chains were made to stand up and move as best they could. By late afternoon the men were sent below, but women and children were allowed on top a little longer, if the weather permitted.

When dark set in, the ship's officers went into the hold to arrange the slaves for sleep. Most slaves slept lying against one another. Of course there was a constant struggle for room— to stretch, to sneeze, to cough,

———

In response to protests against the inhuman conditions aboard slave ships, Britain passed an act in 1788 to control the number of Africans per loading space. This etching of the deck plans for the British slave ship Brookes *shows how 454 slaves were packed like sardines all according to regulation. The plan for figure 2 allows each male slave six feet by sixteen inches, each female five feet by sixteen inches, each boy five feet by fourteen inches and each girl four and one-half feet by twelve inches. It's frightening to imagine the torment of such a voyage.*

———

Dancing on deck.

to scratch. What to do to relieve yourself in the night? Buckets were placed to be used as latrines. But how could chained slaves reach them in the dark? And what did you do if seasickness hit you and you had to vomit?

No wonder people spoke of the unmistakable smell of the slave ships. It seems to have been a stink compounded of sea salt, of excrement, of sweating and terrified bodies, and of the recently dead. No one who sniffed it could ever forget it.

Under such conditions large numbers of slaves fell sick and many died. William Chancellor of Philadelphia, ship surgeon aboard the *Wolf*, made a slaving voyage from New York to Africa in 1750. This ship and two other slavers were owned by Phillip Livingston, a wealthy New York merchant, among those who would sign the Declaration of Independence.

As the *Wolf* sailed out, the surgeon began to record his experiences in a diary. The ship reached Africa in September. It took fourteen months for the *Wolf* to load enough slaves from several stations along the coast to begin the return voyage to New York.

Almost from the time of purchase the surgeon found that sickness had seized several slaves. The small ship's decks were always awash in water, and the slaves were up to their ankles in it. Those many months waiting

In the hold of the slave ship Gloria.

aboard ship for a full cargo meant the slaves had to sit all day in irons, "so cramped that this day," the surgeon wrote in his diary, "I was obliged to bathe seven of their knees with warm water before they could walk."

In May 1750 Chancellor noted that forty-three of the young slaves on the *Wolf* had come down with the measles. When a girl of about five died from the illness, her body was tossed overboard. A day later his diary read:

> This morning early going down among the slaves I found a boy dead, at noon another, and in the afternoon, another. Oh Reader, whoever thou art, it is impossible for you to conceive or me to describe the torture I sustain at the loss of these slaves we have committed to a watery grave.

A few days later:

> Early this morning found a little girl about 3 years old dead, whom I opened immediately and found in her intestines 7 worms, some of them 12 and 13 inches, rolled up together in a bundle. She had the flux and measles.

More and more dead, day after day, each corpse tossed overboard. When he ran out of medical supplies he noted:

> It is a very melancholy prospect to see everybody sick and not have a medicine to help them and the thought of being out six months longer without medicines is a miserable thought. . . . I can give them nothing but good nursing.

Medical science at that time was in a very elementary stage, with few drugs that were effective against disease. Chancellor feared that the loss of so many slaves would bring blame upon him from angry investors who cared nothing for the dead but only for the loss of profit.

Arab planters on the island of Zanzibar might own as many as 2,000 slaves. In the 1840s, twenty to forty thousand slaves were brought to the island each year. They were so badly treated that many neared starvation, as this engraving shows. But if only one out of two survived, the traders still made quite a profit.

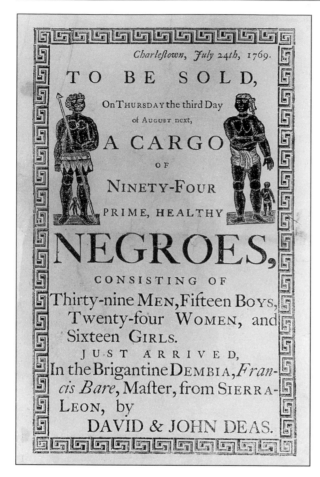

*Broadsides of 1769 and 1829
announced the sale of slaves in
American cities.*

In January 1751 the *Wolf* began her homeward journey. The passage took 113 days. In the fourteen months of slaving, 135 men, women, and children had been purchased. Of these, 60 had died before the Wolf left Africa. Seventy-five slaves began the Middle Passage; two of them died on the voyage home, one of an accident, the other, a boy, of "a long and lingering illness—consumption." The *Wolf* docked in New York on May 10, and three days later the *New York Gazette* published an announcement:

TO BE SOLD on Friday, the 17th Instant, at 10 o'clock in the Morning, at the Meal Market, a Number of likely Negro Slaves,

TO BE SOLD & LET

BY PUBLIC AUCTION,

On MONDAY the 18th of MAY, 1829,

UNDER THE TREES.

FOR SALE,

THE THREE FOLLOWING

SLAVES,

VIZ.

HANNIBAL, about 30 Years old, an excellent House Servant, of Good Character.

WILLIAM, about 35 Years old, a Labourer.

NANCY, an excellent House Servant and Nurse.

The MEN belonging to "LEECH'S" Estate, and the WOMAN to Mrs. D. SMIT

TO BE LET,

On the usual conditions of the Hirer finding them in Food, Clothing, and Medical ance,

THE FOLLOWING

MALE and FEMALE

SLAVES,

OF GOOD CHARACTERS.

ROBERT BAGLEY, about 20 Years old, a good House Servant.

WILLIAM BAGLEY, about 18 Years old, a Labourer.

JOHN ARMS, about 18 Years old.

JACK ANTONIA, about 40 Years old, a Labourer.

PHILIP, an Excellent Fisherman.

HARRY, about 27 Years old, a good House Servant.

LUCY, a Young Woman of good Character, used to House Work and the Nursery.

ELIZA, an Excellent Washerwoman.

CLARA, an Excellent Washerwoman.

FANNY, about 14 Years old, House Servant.

SARAH, about 14 Years old, House Servant.

Also for Sale, at Eleven o'Clock,

Fine Rice, Gram, Paddy, Books, Muslins, Needles, Pins, Ribbons &c. &c.

AT ONE O'CLOCK, THAT CELEBRATED ENGLISH HORSE

BLUCHER,

ADDISON PRINTER GOVERNMENT

What Was the Chance of Survival?

What chance did a slave have—captured or bought on Africa's west coast—to reach the Americas alive?

All voyages were risky, for the science of navigation and the technology of sailing were quite skimpy. Then there were the usual hazards of sailing vessels—storms and calms—and pirates at any time might swoop down to capture the slave cargo. Disease often swept the densely packed vessels, especially when calms or mishaps caused long delays.

On average, the duration of the Middle Passage from West Africa was sixty days. A longer voyage meant reduced food and water, which lowered the resistance to disease of both slaves and crew. In the earlier decades of the trade the death rate was nearly 25 percent: one out of every four slaves died. By the late 1700s it had dropped to about 7 percent. In some periods it varied from about 3 percent to 10 percent. Yet some ships had death rates ranging from 18 percent to an appalling 52 percent. Men died at a somewhat higher rate than women: 19 percent to about 15 percent.

By the end of the slaving era certain changes had occurred that cut down mortality in the trade. Ship design and construction improved, researchers learned more about diseases and how to treat them, and doctors provided better hygiene aboard ship to reduce the toll. If profit was the aim of selling a product, why destroy it?

lately imported in the Sloop *Wolf* directly from Africa. Those that are not disposed of on that Day, will be sold the Friday following.

On occasion, at the last moment, when land was again in sight, some of the Africans would make a last desperate attempt to escape. In 1737 as the slaver *Prince of Orange* anchored in the harbor of St. Kitts in the Caribbean, more than one hundred slaves jumped over the side. The captain reported:

Out of the whole, we lost 33 as good men slaves as we had on board, who would not endeavor to save themselves, but resolved to die, and sunk directly down. Many more of them were taken up almost drowned. Some of them died since, but not the owners' loss, they being sold before any discovery was made of the injury the salt water had done them. . . .

What choice did the African have? To die? Or to revolt?

Mutiny aboard a slave ship. The armed crew fires at the rebelling slaves from the barricaded quarterdeck. William Snelgrave, a veteran slaver, wrote a book in 1734 describing several mutinies he had witnessed or heard about. He offered advice to slave ship captains on how to avoid mutinies or, if they broke out, how to put them down.

Five

Better to Die—
or to Revolt?

SLAVES WHO NO LONGER WISHED TO LIVE OFTEN FOUND SOME WAY TO end their suffering. Women twisted their cotton skirts into rope to hang themselves. Men and women tried to starve themselves and were severely whipped so that they would eat. If they still refused, a device was used to force food down their throats. Not even that worked, if the slave spit it out or vomited it up. It enraged captains when a slave tried to die by starvation. For every slave that died aboard ship the investors lost the price they might have gotten if the slave had been brought to market.

One slave leaped overboard when crewmen were not watching, only to find that in spite of himself he was swimming. Determined to die, he pulled his cotton waistcloth over his head and sank beneath the waves.

Slaves were known to die of melancholy. It happened over and over again. If one slave set his mind on dying, it spread like wildfire. "When one dies, others will follow," seamen said.

As a ship left the slaves' home shore it could bring on suicidal attempts. The slaves became desperate, and even with shackles fixed, would throw themselves over the side. Weighed down by the iron, they would go underwater before a boat could be lowered to haul them up.

Many more were determined to live rather than die—and go free. The fear of slave mutinies led to strict controls, and any attempt to rebel was savagely punished. Every slave welcomed the chance to escape. Some groups of people, such as the Coromantees of the Gold Coast, were especially feared for their pride and their mutinous behavior. The crews on slavers always kept their whips in their hands and their guns on their belts. The threat of a slave uprising was ever present, particularly when ships remained near the African coast. A mutiny when land was in sight offered the slaves a more likely escape. Crews would inspect the holds daily, looking into every corner and hole for pieces of iron, wood, or knives hidden by the slaves. Nothing must be left around that could be picked up by a slave and used as a weapon.

The yearning to return to their homeland led slaves to rise up for freedom. One such attempt was made on the *Wolf* as she lay off the coast of Africa. Secretly armed with cutlasses by the second mate, who sought revenge upon the captain he hated, the slaves revolted, and a bloody battle was fought with the crew. The captain, the surgeon, and others were wounded, but the slaves were overcome. A few managed to get away in a small boat, only to be captured by seamen from another slaver.

In 1700 John Casseneuve, first mate of the *Don Carlos* out of London, witnessed a revolt on his ship and reported how it happened. The slaves had been eating their noon meal:

Most of them were yet above deck, many of them provided with knives, which we had indiscreetly given them two or three days before, as not suspecting the least attempt of this nature from them. Others had pieces of iron they had torn off our forecastle door. Having premeditated a revolt, and seeing all the ship's company, at best but weak and many quite sick, they had also broken off the shackles from several of their companions' feet. Which served them, as well as billets they had provided themselves with, and all other things they could lay hands on, which they imagined might be of use for their enterprise.

Thus armed, they fell in crowds and parcels on our men, upon the deck unawares, and stabbed one of the stoutest of us all, who received fourteen or fifteen wounds of their knives, and so expired. Next they assaulted our boatswain, and cut one of his legs so round the bone, that he could not move, the nerves being cut through. Others cut our cook's throat to the pipe, and others wounded three of the sailors, and threw one of them overboard in that condition, from the forecastle into the sea, who, however, by Providence, got hold, of the bowline of the foresail, and saved himself. . . .

We stood in arms, firing on the revolted slaves, of whom we killed some, and wounded many. Which terrified the rest, that they gave way. . . . Many of the most mutinous leaped overboard, and drowned themselves in the ocean with much resolution, showing no manner of concern for life. Thus we lost 27 or 28 slaves, either killed by us, or drowned, and having mastered them, caused all to go betwixt decks, giving them good words.

In 1750 a Boston newspaper reported a revolt at sea when a Liverpool ship with 350 slaves aboard came in sight of the Caribbean island of Guadeloupe. As the slaves were brought up on deck for air, he said, they seized an opportunity

. . . and killed the master and mate of the ship, and threw 15 of the men overboard, after which they sent the boat with two white lads and three or four others to discover what land it was. Meanwhile

Crushing a mutiny the crew toss overboard the slaves who would rather die than give in.

the ship drove to the leeward, which gave the lads an opportunity to discover the affair to the commandant of that quarter of the island, who immediately raised about 100 men, and put them on board a sloop, who went in pursuit of the ship, and in a few hours took her and carried her into Port Louis.

Early in the eighteenth century John Atkins recorded the punishment meted out to rebels on the *Robert* of Bristol:

Captain Harding, weighing the stoutness and worth [of the ringleaders] did, as in other countries they do by rogues of dignity, whip and scarify them only; while three other abettors, but not actors, nor of strength for it, he sentenced to cruel deaths, making them first eat the heart and liver of one of them killed. The woman he hoisted up by the thumbs, whipped, and slashed at her with knives, before the other slaves, until she died.

The most famous slave mutiny—and it was successful—occurred on the *Amistad*. Early in 1839 Portuguese slavers had loaded 733 captives on the West African coast for shipment to the slave markets of Cuba. One of the captives was Joseph Cinqué, kidnapped from the rice fields where he worked. When the ship disembarked in Havana, fifty-two days later, only 188 slaves were counted. All the rest had died at sea.

At Havana, Cinqué and the others were bought by two Spaniards, who chartered the schooner *Amistad* to carry their human cargo to Puerto Príncipe, a Cuban town where they would be sold. At night below deck Cinqué found a nail, which he used to break the lock on his iron collar.

Joseph Cinqué, leader of the Amistad *mutiny, painted from life by Nathaniel Jocelyn in New Haven, Connecticut. "What a master spirit is his," wrote the abolitionist poet Whittier. "What a soul for the tyrant to crush down in bondage."*

How Many Were Enslaved?

The number of Africans enslaved in the mass migration to the Americas has been a subject of some debate. No exact records were kept during those four hundred years, and many nations were involved. Still, modern scholars have collected a vast amount of data and have expended great effort to reach a reasonable estimate.

Philip D. Curtin did pioneering work in the field, publishing his study, *The African Slave Trade: A Census*, in 1969. Following up on his work, Paul Lovejoy came close to the same findings. He estimated that Africa exported some 11,698,000 people and that 9,778,500 landed in the Americas. Almost two million lost their lives in the crossing.

Then he freed the others. They seized weapons from the sleeping crew and killed the captain and cook.

With Cinqué in command, the Africans tied the two Spaniards to the bridge and ordered them to steer the ship toward Africa. (The white sailors were not killed but set adrift in a small boat.)

But the Spaniards, aware that the Africans knew nothing about navigation, tricked them by steering north and west during the night instead

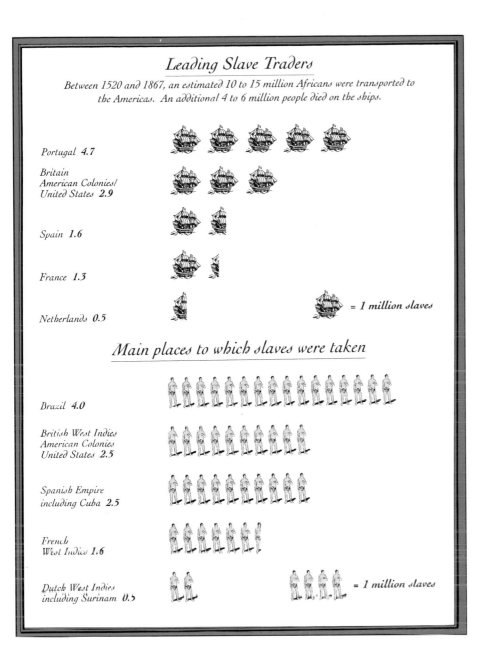

Leading Slave Traders

Between 1520 and 1867, an estimated 10 to 15 million Africans were transported to the Americas. An additional 4 to 6 million people died on the ships.

Portugal **4.7**

Britain
American Colonies/
United States **2.9**

Spain **1.6**

France **1.3**

Netherlands **0.5**

= 1 million slaves

Main places to which slaves were taken

Brazil **4.0**

British West Indies
American Colonies
United States **2.5**

Spanish Empire
including Cuba **2.5**

French
West Indies **1.6**

Dutch West Indies
including Surinam **0.5**

= 1 million slaves

of east and south. For sixty-three days they zigzagged. Desperate from thirst and lack of food, ten of the Africans died before the *Amistad* beached on Long Island. There, a brig of the U.S. Navy sighted the strange ship and sent sailors aboard to learn its business. They were astonished to find only Africans in charge. At pistol point they ordered all hands below deck. The *Amistad* was convoyed not to New York, where slavery had been abolished, but to New London, Connecticut,

The death of Captain Ferrer, as the Africans captured command of the Amistad *off the Cuban coast in July 1839.*

where slavery was still legal. The Africans were charged with murder and jailed to await trial.

Abolitionists formed a committee to raise funds for the defense of the Africans. At trial, young Cinqué made so passionate a speech in court that, though no one could understand his language, it helped swing the court in the Africans' favor. A judge ruled that the blacks had been kidnapped in Africa in violation of laws against the slave trade, and that their mutiny was justified to prevent enslavement.

When U.S. president Martin Van Buren, eager to please Southern voters in the upcoming election of 1840, sought to deliver the blacks to Cuba for trial, the abolitionists took the case to the Supreme Court. Then John Quincy Adams, the former U.S. president, now a Massachusetts congressman, stepped in. He was so moved by the plight of the captives that, weak and almost sightless at the age of seventy-three, he nevertheless appealed on their behalf in a nearly five-hour speech before the Court. On March 9, 1841, the Court ruled that the Africans should be freed and allowed to return to their homeland.

In 1841 another mutiny occurred, this time on the *Creole*, sailing from Virginia for New Orleans. While at sea, 130 slaves rebelled, killed a slave owner, and steered the ship into the harbor of Nassau in the Bahamas, where, under British law, they were freed.

How frequent were slave uprisings on the ships? For the years between 1690 and 1845 the historian Daniel Mannix found detailed reports of fifty-five slave revolts aboard ship and references to one hundred more. At least as many slave ships were wrecked and plundered in port or offshore by Africans who attacked them and roughed up the crew. When slave trade investors reduced the size of their crews to make more money, those ships were easier targets for mutineers. But revolts did little to limit the trade, and profit-hungry slavers continued to pack their cargoes of wretched human beings into ships' holds without regard for the pain they inflicted on the body and the spirit.

John Quincy Adams, sixth president of the United States and later a congressman from Massachusetts, argued the case of the African mutineers before the Supreme Court and won their freedom.

Twenty Africans from Guinea—fourteen men and six women—who were transported on a Dutch slave ship land in the colony of Jamestown, Virginia, in 1619. Painting by Howard Pyle.

Six

Enslaved in the Americas

THE AFRICANS WHO SURVIVED THE MIDDLE PASSAGE AND LANDED IN THE Americas alive were ticketed for sale a second time. The number of slaves imported from Africa is not known for certain. The best estimate holds that it was about 12 million. The forced mass migration brought slaves to Brazil, Colombia, Argentina, Peru, Mexico, and Panama as well as to the Caribbean. From these points they were forwarded to where the European colonists needed them.

The slave ships carried Africans to colonial North America late in the trade's history. It was 1619 when a Dutch ship entered Jamestown in the colony of Virginia and sold twenty slaves in exchange for food and goods. By that time a million blacks had already been brought from Africa to South America and the Caribbean. But not until 1730, when staple agriculture—such crops as cotton, rice, and tobacco—began to spread, did North America import sizable numbers of slaves. The years from 1730 to the outbreak of the American Revolution saw a surge of imports. By 1776 the slave population had climbed to more than 500,000. Most of the slaves came directly from Africa. The largest number—two out of three—were sold by English traders. For in the eighteenth century, England was at the forefront of the slave trade.

American traders, without any posts in Africa, used the English posts. Rhode Island was the colony most active in the slave trade. Her ships made about one thousand voyages to Africa and in one century brought over 100,000 slaves to the New World. New York, Massachusetts, and Pennsylvania actively plied the trade as well.

Relatively few slaves were brought to the northern colonies because they had no large-scale farming requiring mass labor. The slave ships owned by northerners carried the Africans to the West Indies or to the southern colonies.

In the New World the slaves' primary use was on the vast estates of the West Indies, in the southern regions of North America, and in Latin America—wherever mass labor was in demand.

Yet even before the first African slaves reached the New World, there were slaves already at work. Do you remember how the Europeans encountered slaves when their ships touched African shores? They also found slavery among the Native Americans when they sailed along the coasts of North and South America. The Aztecs of Central America had taken slaves by war or raiding, and made certain crimes punishable by enslavement. Among the Maya of Central America a man could sell himself or his children into slavery. Along the northwest coast of North America, south from present-day Alaska to northern California, Indians valued slaves as a mark of personal wealth or rank.

The smaller Indian tribes were raided whenever stronger tribes wanted captives to sell as slaves. Slave raiding was common too among the Indians of southwestern North America. Across the continent, prisoners of war were made slaves for life. They were used for whatever tasks

How Did the Slave Trade Affect West Africa?

Four hundred years of the Atlantic slave trade had profound effects upon West Africa. It brought disaster to its peoples. Millions of young men and women, upon whose efforts the development of any region depends, were lost to slavery. Local industries, such as gold mining, could no longer be pursued in peace. The introduction of firearms in great quantity led to the collapse of the traditional order and the subjugation of peoples. Tribal groups and states were caught up in the terrible practice of conducting raids on their weaker neighbors or selling their own people in order to feed the slave market and thus gain the European products they had come to desire for pleasure and to make themselves more powerful. There was slavery before the Europeans came, but it carried none of the racist burden that developed in the Americas. There can be little doubt that the Atlantic slave trade perverted West Africa's social system, distorted its political order, and hampered its economic growth.

their masters demanded of them. As we have seen, in every society the rich and the powerful have enslaved the poor or the helpless.

Hundreds and often thousands of African slaves in the Americas worked together to raise sugar, cotton, coffee, rice, tobacco, maize, and cacao for their masters. Slaves worked too on big ranches, in mines, in shops, on the docks, and in homes.

Such labor required physical strength and endurance. But other tasks assigned to slaves made intellectual demands or required the ingenious skills of the artisan. On plantations in both North and South America, the richer the planter the more domestic slaves he used, and the more specialized were their tasks. A wealthy planter's home would be full of cooks, butlers, waiters, footmen, coachmen, hostlers, laundresses, chambermaids, and nursemaids.

Plantation labor under the eye of the overseer, who is armed with gun and whip.

Carting sugar in the West Indies for shipment abroad. Enslavement in Africa was linked to sugar production in the Americas. The slave traders prospered along with the sugar producers.

In the towns and cities of the American South, most of the domestic work was done by enslaved women. Some slaves became expert brick masons, carpenters, and ironworkers. They built many of our stately mansions and imposing public buildings.

Domestic work by slaves made for ease and comfort but did not add to a master's wealth. Most masters put their slaves to work that brought in profits. Slaves worked on the plantations first of all. But they also worked as mechanics and wagoners; they built canals and railroads, and manned tobacco factories, ironworks, sugar refineries, rice and flour mills,

Rice culture on the Ogeechee River near Savannah, Georgia, in the 1800s. It was drudgery of the worst kind, performed under the worst conditions. Rice production required the heaviest concentration of slaves anywhere in the South. A highly profitable business, it resulted in a terrible death rate among slaves.

and cotton presses. Some masters hired out their slaves to other people.

Slaveholding was less suited to the small family farms and local manufacturing of the northern states. It died out gradually, although northern shipowners continued making money from the slave trade. But slavery persisted and expanded in the South. The invention of the cotton gin (a machine that culled the seeds and foreign material from cotton) in 1793 enlarged profits from enslaved agricultural labor. Slavery soon became the basis of the southern way of life. By 1860—just before the Civil War began—there were well over three million slaves in the South.

The majority were producing the five great staple crops—cotton, tobacco, sugar, rice, and indigo.

What was their work like? The daily task of a slave in the cotton fields was described by Solomon Northup, a slave who told his story after his escape in 1853. From "day clean to first dark," he said, the slaves stayed in the fields:

The hands are required to be in the cotton field as soon as it is light in the morning, and, with the exception of ten or fifteen min-

Eli Whitney, a Yankee schoolteacher, visiting the South in 1792, was told by cotton planters how hard it was to gin cotton by hand. Within six months he invented a machine—shown in this wood engraving—to clean the cotton of its seeds far more efficiently. His invention did much to change the South's economy.

utes, which is given them at noon to swallow their allowance of cold bacon, they are not permitted to be a moment idle until it is too dark to see and when the moon is full they often-times labor till the middle of the night. They do not dare to stop even at dinner time, nor return to the quarters, however late it be, until the order to halt is given by the driver.

The day's work over in the field, the baskets are "toted" or in other words carried to the ginhouse, where the cotton is weighed. No matter how fatigued and weary he may be—no matter how much he longs for sleep and rest—a slave never approaches the ginhouse with his basket of cotton but with fear. If it falls short in weight—if he has not performed the full task appointed him—he knows that he must suffer. And if he has exceeded it by ten or twenty pounds, in all probability his master will measure the next day's task accordingly.

So, whether he has too little or too much, his approach to the ginhouse is always with fear and trembling. Most frequently they have too little, and therefore it is they are not anxious to leave the fields. After weighing, follow the whippings; and then the baskets are carried to the cotton house, and their contents stored away like hay, all hands being sent in to tramp it down.

But that by no means ended the day, said Northup:

Each one must then attend to his respective chores. One feeds the mules, another the swine—another cuts the wood, and so forth; besides, the packing is all done by candle light. Finally, at a late hour, they reach the quarters, sleepy and overcome with the long day's toil. Then a fire must be kindled in the cabin, the corn ground in a small hand-mill, and supper, and dinner for the next day in the field, prepared.

As cotton production rose to supply textile mills in England and the North, more and more land was put into cotton and more slaves were bought to raise the crop. Cotton soon became king—it was the leading crop and chief export product. By 1850 nearly two million slaves were engaged in its production.

No matter what the crop, the field hands were driven to the breaking point day after day, year after year. Their hours often ran to sixteen or eighteen a day. They were treated like "an animal tool" to produce the highest profit.

No wonder slavery could pay off handsomely for some masters. James Madison, a Virginia slave owner who would become the fourth president of the United States, said he could make $257 a year on each slave, while spending only about $12 a year on his keep.

How did that abuse of human beings jibe with the claim of the Declaration of Independence to "life, liberty and the pursuit of happiness" for all Americans? Speaking to an antislavery audience of whites on the Fourth of July in 1852, the ex-slave Frederick Douglass thundered a challenge to America's hypocritical democracy:

W hat to the American slave is your Fourth of July? I answer, a day that reveals to him more than all other days of the year, the gross injustice and cruelty to which he is the constant victim. To him your celebration is a sham; your boasted liberty an unholy license;

Frederick Douglass, the most renowned and influential black leader of the nineteenth century. Born a slave in Maryland in 1818, he escaped to freedom and by an iron will, hard work, and great talent helped to win his people's liberation.

your national greatness, swelling vanity; your sounds of rejoicing are empty and heartless; your denunciation of tyrants, brass-fronted impudence; your shouts of liberty and equality, hollow mockery; your prayers and hymns, your sermons and thanksgivings, with all your religious parade and solemnity, are to him mere bombast, fraud, deception, impiety, and hypocrisy—a thin veil to cover up crimes which would disgrace a nation of savages. There is not a nation of the earth guilty of practices more shocking and bloody than are the people of these United States at this very hour.

Go where you may, search where you will, roam through all the monarchies and despotisms of the Old World, travel through South America, search out every abuse and when you have found the last, lay your facts by the side of the everyday practices of this nation, and you will say with me that, for revolting barbarity and shameless hypocrisy, America reigns without a rival.

Yet the slaves struggled to make a livable world for themselves and their children. The law viewed them as things, as nonhumans. But they were human. They did think and dream. They were imaginative and inventive. They created their own family life, folk religion, music, stories, and art. They shaped ways to express themselves. They learned how to endure.

This, in a democracy that was birthed upon slavery. In 1776 the colonial leaders signed the Declaration of Independence, which proclaimed that "all men are created equal." How deeply did the Founding Fathers believe it? Were the people who happened to be black not entitled to "life, liberty and the pursuit of happiness?" That question troubled many, such as Thomas Jefferson and George Washington, slave owners themselves.

It is hard to live with a troubled conscience. But the slave masters of that time found a way to ease their minds. In Europe, and in America too, they developed an excuse for slavery—an excuse called racism. It is the mistaken belief, developed over a great many centuries, that one race

In this lithograph of 1853, George Washington is shown directing slaves on his plantation. When the Revolution began he owned 135 slaves. But feeling qualms about slavery, he stopped buying them; moreover, he would not sell those he owned without their permission, which not one would give. In his will he arranged for the freedom of all his slaves after the death of his wife, Martha. (He was the only one of the Virginia Founding Fathers to do so.)

is superior to people of any other color. And that this superior people have the right to rule others. That racist belief—shared by many of the Founding Fathers—made it easy to justify the enslavement of blacks. Even though Jefferson and others like him were troubled by the question of slavery, they rarely took a stand against it, or tried to change the slave system. Yes, slavery was a crime, but somehow they could find no way to destroy it. They were not willing to give up their human property, their comfortable way of life, or their political influence by actively opposing slavery.

The fighting in the Revolutionary War broke out at Lexington and Concord. The artist shows the black American called Salem shooting Major Pitcairn, a British officer. About 30,000 slaves in the South, Jefferson estimated, fled their owners in the hope of finding freedom with the British.

When the war with Britain was won, the colonists had both their independence and their slaves. The men who wrote the new Constitution did not end slavery. In fact, they prohibited Congress from halting the foreign slave trade before 1808. With that deadline facing them, there was a rush by the slave traders to import more slaves.

It did not seem to matter that five thousand blacks had helped win the fight for independence. Sadly, the leaders of the Revolution had a narrow idea of the concept of freedom. Nor did the nation as a whole raise a hand against slavery. The failure of the Founding Fathers left a moral legacy that has done harm to the generations that have come after. They too have compromised and temporized on the principles of liberty we claim are the foundation of our way of life. That is why racial segregation and discrimination are not accidental in American history. They are part of a long heritage.

The closing of the African slave trade did not prove to be the first step toward the abolition of slavery. For just at the time the foreign supply was officially being cut off, slavery was stretching past the limits of the original Southern states. One by one, new territories—Kentucky, Tennessee, Mississippi, Alabama—entered the Union as slave states.

So, in spite of the law banning the slave trade in 1808, slavers continued to bring Africans into the United States. Even when a federal law of 1820 made slaving punishable by death as piracy, the illegal trade continued right up to the beginning of the Civil War.

In all, it is estimated that 600,000 slaves were imported into the present United States. About one third of that vast involuntary migration occurred in the last two decades of the lawful trade.

By the mid-1820s, however, American slave buyers depended far more on the high birthrate of their own country's slaves and on a flourishing domestic trade to supply their needs. That was one of the worst features of slavery in the prewar South. To the forced migration of Africans on the Middle Passage it added the forced migration of a large

A slave market in Atlanta, Georgia, photographed during the Civil War years. Slaves were sold in stores such as these, along with cheeses, clocks, crockery, old books, pickles, shoes—anything. Bidders for slaves would step up to examine the merchandise, telling them to walk back and forth to see if they were lame—much as a butcher would inspect a calf for sale.

An illustration from about 1890, showing four generations of an African-American family, all born on the plantation of J. J. Smith in Beaufort, South Carolina.

number of blacks in an interstate slave trade. Professional slave traders made profits from the increasing demand for forced labor in the expanding cotton and sugar plantations of the Old Southwest.

The traders advertised in the newspapers, offering to pay the best prices for slaves. So big a business did it become that a slave trader might deal for five thousand slaves in just one season. Slaves were bought individually or in small groups, often as a family. But families were broken up, too, sold apart from one another, never to meet again.

In some slave societies, but rarely in America, slaves were allowed to purchase their freedom. Even then, the vast majority could not earn the necessary money. No wonder they were a "troublesome property" to their masters. Some ran away, some damaged tools and crops, some burned down buildings, some stole to keep from going hungry, some did as little as possible on the job.

Flight was the route to freedom, the only way out. And thousands, usually the younger people, fled every year. It was, like sabotage, proof of how fiercely bondage was hated and independence prized.

Every slave who ran free was living proof to all the others that they were not doomed to slavery until death. The slaveholders did everything possible to forestall escapes and to recover runaways. Still, 75,000 slaves got away to freedom in the fifty years before the Civil War ended slavery.

Masters lived in fear of murder or revolt. And with good reason. Some slaves did kill their masters. There were many plots to revolt, although none succeeded. One was led by Gabriel Prosser of Virginia in 1800 and another by Denmark Vesey of South Carolina in 1822. Both failed and their leaders were executed. A third, led by Nat Turner of Virginia in 1831, terrified the whole South. It took troops three days to put down the rebellion, during which fifty-eight whites were killed. Turner and sixteen of his followers were hanged.

Many people profited hugely from slavery and the slave trade. They found it hard to act against their own selfish interests. It was outside the centers of slavery that the movement to abolish it took root. As the number of freed black people grew in the early 1800s, from their ranks came many leaders of the abolition movement. Frederick Douglass was foremost among them. White abolitionists such as William Lloyd Garrison, Wendell Phillips, the Grimké sisters, and John Brown joined them. They wrote, preached, lectured, and organized for the cause of black freedom. Often they met with bitter and violent opposition, in the North as well as in the South. They turned to politics too, electing anti-slavery candidates to office.

Although more and more men and women enlisted in the slavery cause, and succeeded in spreading their message wide, their peaceful efforts to end the curse of slavery were not enough. When Abraham Lincoln, who had pledged himself to end the expansion of slavery, took office in 1861, the Southern slaveholding states left the Union. The Civil War followed, with the North determined to preserve the Union. But the war rapidly developed into a war to crush slavery. The Emancipation Proclamation of January 1, 1863, was the turning point. And when the Confederate army was defeated in 1865, three amendments to the Constitution confirmed the battlefield decision: the thirteenth abolished slavery, the fourteenth protected the rights of blacks as citizens, and the fifteenth their right to vote.

So slavery in the United States finally died.

But in other parts of the world it lives, sometimes in forms intended to mask its real nature. If all governments would decide to abolish slavery and to enforce their laws, slavery could be ended everywhere. And so could the forced mass migration of people. To accomplish this, governments must be encouraged, aided, or shamed into taking action to protect human liberty and freedom of movement. Only then can all of us be assured that we are truly free.

Bibliography

The Bibliography lists scholarly sources on slavery and the slave trade. Most are in print, or are available in public and university libraries. I owe much to the work of these historians.

In the Further Reading, I list some novels for young readers, which portray aspects of the slave experience. Good fiction can add another dimension to our understanding of history.

Aitken, Hugh G. J. *Did Slavery Pay?* Boston: Houghton Mifflin, 1971.

Atmore, Anthony and Gillian Stacey. *Black Kingdoms, Black Peoples: The West African Heritage.* London: Orbis, 1979.

Balandier, Georges. *Daily Life in the Kingdom of the Kongo; From the 16th to the 18th Century.* New York: Meridian, 1969.

Blackburn, Robin. *The Making of New World Slavery, 1492–1800.* New York: Verso, 1998.

Curtin, Philip D., ed. *Africa Remembered: Narratives by West Africans from the Era of the Slave Trade.* Madison, WI: University of Wisconsin Press, 1967.

The Atlantic Slave Trade: A Census. Madison, WI: University of Wisconsin Press, 1972.

Davidson, Basil, ed. *African Civilization Revisited.* Lawrenceville, NJ: Red Sea Press, 1990.

Davidson, Basil. *The African Slave Trade*. Boston: Little Brown, 1988.

Davis, David Brion. *The Problem of Slavery in Western Culture*. New York: Oxford University Press, 1988.

Donnan, Elizabeth, ed. *Documents Illustrative of the History of the Slave Trade to America*. 4 vols. Washington, DC: Smithsonian, 1930–35.

Equiano, Olaudah. *The Interesting Narrative of the Life of Olaudah Equiano, or Gustavus Vassa, the African*. New York: Longmans, 1988.

Everett, Susanne. *History of Slavery*. Edison, NJ: Chartwell House, 1996.

Franklin, John Hope. *Race and History*. Baton Rouge, LA: Louisiana State University Press, 1990.

Gardner, Brian. *The African Dream*. New York: Putnam, 1970.

Greene, Lorenzo J. *The Negro in Colonial New England*. New York: Atheneum, 1968.

Herskovits, Melville J., ed. *The New World Negro*. Bloomington: Indiana University Press, 1966.

Howard, Richard. *Black Cargo*. New York: Putnam, 1972.

Huggins, Nathan Irvin. *Black Odyssey: The African American Ordeal in Slavery*. New York: Vintage, 1990.

Jones, Howard. *Mutiny on the Amistad*. New York: Oxford, 1997.

Jordan, Winthrop D. *White Over Black: American Attitudes Toward the Negro, 1550–1812*. Williamsburg, VA: Institute of Early American History and Culture, 1995.

Katz, William Loren. *Eyewitness: A Living Documentary of the African American Contribution to American History*. New York: Touchstone, 1995.

Knapton, Ernest John. *Europe: 1450–1815*. New York: Scribner's, 1958.

Meltzer, Milton. *The Black Americans: A History in Their Own Words*. New York: HarperCollins, 1984.

Slavery: A World History. New York: Da Capo, 1993.

Miller, Randall M., and John David Smith. *Dictionary of Afro-American Slavery*. Westport, CT: Praeger, 1997.

Owens, William A. *Black Mutiny: The Revolt on the Schooner Amistad*. New York: Plume, 1997.

Parry, J. H. *The Age of Reconnaissance*. Berkeley, CA: University of California Press, 1982.

Pietersen Jan Nederveen. *White on Black: Images of Africa and Blacks in Western Popular Culture*. New Haven, CT: Yale University Press, 1992.

Plumb, J. H. *England in the 18th Century*. New York: Penguin, 1990.

Pope-Hennesey, James. *The Sins of the Fathers: A Study of the Atlantic Slave Trade: 1440–1807*. New York: Barnes and Noble, 1998.

Reynolds, Edward. *Stand the Storm: A History of the Atlantic Slave Trade*. London: Willison & Bisbo, 1985.

Thomas, Hugh. *The Slave Trade: The Story of the Atlantic Slave Trade: 1440–1870*. New York: Touchstone, 1999.

Thomas, Velma Maia. *Lest We Forget: The Passage from Africa to Slavery and Emancipation*. New York: Crown, 1997.

Ungar, Sanford J. *Africa*. New York: Touchstone, 1989.

Unsworth, Barry. *Sacred Hunger*. New York: W. W. Norton, 1993.

Ward, W.E.F. *The Royal Navy and the Slavers*. New York: Pantheon, 1969.

Wax, Darold D. "A Philadelphia Surgeon on a Slaving Voyage to Africa, 1749–1751." *Pennsylvania Magazine of History and Biography*. V. 92, 1968, 465–493.

Further Reading

FICTION

Burchard, Peter. *Chinwe*. New York: Putnam, 1979.

Fox, Paula. *The Slave Dancer*. New York: Yearling, 1991.

Meltzer, Milton. *Underground Man*. San Diego: Harcourt Brace, 1990.

Sterne, Emma G. *The Slave Ship*. New York: Scholastic, 1975.

Paulsen, Gary. *Nightjohn*. New York: Delacorte, 1993.

Turner, Glennette T., *Running for Our Lives*. New York: Holiday House, 1994.

Lyons, Mary. *Letters from a Slave Girl: The Story of Harriet Jacob*. New York: Atheneum, 1992.

NONFICTION

Fleischner, Jennifer. *I Was Born a Slave: The Story of Harriet Jacobs*. Brookfield, CT: Millbrook, 1997.

Hamilton, Virginia. *Many Thousand Gone: African Americans from Slavery to Freedom*. New York: Knopf, 1993.

Hansen, Joyce. *Which Way Freedom?* New York: Camelot, 1992.

Lester, Julius. *To Be a Slave*. New York: Dial Books for Young Readers, 1998.

Ofosu-Appiah, L. H. *People in Bondage*. Minneapolis: Runestone, 1993.

Meltzer, Milton. *All Times, All People: A World History of Slavery*. New York: HarperCollins, 1980.

Index